**DANNY BYRNE**

**GUIDE AND GROW**

The Essential Guide on How to Successfully Guide
Your Child to Grow Up as a Latchkey Kid

Descrierea CIP a Bibliotecii Naționale a României
**DANNY BYRNE**
  **GUIDE AND GROW. The Essential Guide on How to Successfully Guide Your Child to Grow Up as a Latchkey Kid** / Danny Byrne – Bucharest: Editura My Ebook, 2021
    ISBN

**DANNY BYRNE**

# GUIDE AND GROW

**The Essential Guide on How to Successfully Guide Your Child to Grow Up as a Latchkey Kid**

My Ebook Publishing House
Bucharest, 2021

*All over the US, children are going home after school and spending time alone until their parents get home from work. This is what a latchkey kid is. The term came about because they have their own key, usually on a chain hung from their neck, to unlock their home each day when they're done with school.*

*They typically have no adult supervision for two to three hours each evening while they wait for their parents to come home. There are more than four million grade-school-aged latchkey kids because there are a lot of dual-income parents and single parents in the workforce today. But this number is down from its high in the 80s when over half of all children were latchkey kids.*

*It's very difficult to find affordable childcare for this age group. However, before you choose to let your child become a latchkey kid, there are many things to consider - such as the laws in your area, whether your child is mature enough, and your own financial and emotional situation.*

**Latchkey Kids and the Law**

If you're considering letting your child become a latchkey kid, then you need to find out what the law is in your state, city, and county. For the most part, allowing a child to stay home before the age of 8 is not recommended or even legal today. It was done in the past with great regularity but now the laws have changed the rules for parents.

Most professionals agree that children between ages 8 and 10 shouldn't be home alone for more than a couple of hours. Ages 11 to 12 can be home longer but should not be left alone late at night. Kids 13 to 15 can be alone at night, but not all night long. Between 16 and 17 years of age, being left overnight a couple nights is okay. But, keep in mind that your decisions should be made based on the law in your area and the maturity of your child.

**Dangers of Being Latchkey**

Let's be clear before we continue. There are some inherent dangers in being a latchkey kid. But you can mitigate each of them if you're honest about it and aware. Sometimes you have no choice but to take risks, but when you know what the true issues are, you can at least get in front of them and help your child come out on top.

### *Loneliness, Boredom and Fear*

Many studies show one of the biggest problems with latchkey kids is that they are often lonely, bored, and even afraid. That's why it's so important to set up ways to mitigate these issues. Children who have these problems are more likely to fall for those who seek to prey on children through the internet and other means. Talk to your child about stranger (and even relative) danger, and proper behavior that adults should have around kids.

### *Problems with Peer Pressure*

Children starting about middle-school age who spend more than three hours a day alone tend to fall for peer pressure more. They also tend to be more likely to be involved with drug and alcohol use and even sexual activity, due to not following the rules you set about not having friends over. If you never check in or show up unannounced, they will learn that they can get away with it and since their frontal lobes aren't closed yet, they may make bad choices.

### *Sexual Promiscuity and Behavior Problems*

Children left alone for long periods of time tend to suffer from sexual promiscuity and even behavior problems more often than children who aren't. But, many children left alone don't, so there has to be a way to prevent this issue. Open communication, double checking on your kids, and asking others like a trusted neighbor to tell you what's going on can help.

Many children who are latchkey kids also seem to have more issues with conduct disorders and have more issues academically. However, some of this is traced to parents not having time to spend with their kids or money to spend on tutors, health experts, and so forth. If you are aware in advance of this problem, you can know what to watch for in your latchkey child.

### **Benefits of Being a Latchkey Kid**

Now that you're probably scared to death, it's time to make it clear that when done right, there are many benefits to being a latchkey kid. Not all children fall for predators, use drugs, or have sex too early just because they're latchkey kids. Often, there are other issues at play aside from only being a latchkey kid, such as poor parental communication, authoritarian-based parenting, and even drug and alcohol use by parents.

Many children who are latchkey kids thrive because they know their parents love and trust them.

### *Develop Independence*

Many latchkey kids develop independence early, which means that their transition to college or the workforce is a lot easier. Making good choices and having the opportunity to make good choices pays off later in life.

### *Learn Responsibility*

A child who stays home alone learns to be responsible from experience. It's so much better for someone to learn responsibility younger than have it thrust on them all of a sudden once they're an adult. Small increments of responsibility pay off through gaining confidence that can only be learned from experience.

### *Practice Adulting*

So many 18-year-old young adults go off to college or enter the workforce not having a clue about anything to do with adulting. Many can't even make a grilled cheese sandwich or wash a load of laundry - much less write a check or show up to work on time. This is not a good thing for society or the child. Letting them practice and make mistakes, while under the protection of parents, is better.

## *Build Self-Esteem*

Self-esteem is an interesting thing that can only be built through experience. It's not built by someone saying "good job"; it's built by knowing you made a good choice and experiencing the rewards of the great choice. You can't do that if you don't have reasons to make choices on your own.

## *Close Relationships with Parents*

Most latchkey kids have good relationships with their parents as they age. Their relationship is built on mutual respect, not authoritarianism. This doesn't mean you don't make rules. It's just that you make rules and explain them and demonstrate why the rule is important, rather than having a "do as I say or you get punished" method which leads to children having no self-control when not around the parent.

These benefits are multiplied when you are good at communicating with your children, check in with them often, and reason with your kids rather than setting authoritarian rules that need punishments to back them up. In other words, your child follows your rules not to talk to strangers or not to tell strangers on the phone that they're alone. This is because the rule makes sense due to your explanation, not because they're fearful of your punishments.

## Maturity Cues That Show Your Child Is Latchkey Ready

The truth is, no one really wants to leave their young kids home unsupervised. But sometimes life just has its own ideas. Work issues, activities for other kids, and transportation issues, along with the expense of trying to find childcare, can all add up to the need to set your child up as a latchkey kid. But, the first thing you really need to consider is whether your child is mature enough to be a latchkey kid. Look for these signs that signal maturity.

### *They're Not Afraid*

If your child is fearful of staying home alone, then you probably don't want to let them do it yet. Instead, start talking about it so that you can start working on preparing them to let go of their fears if you have any hope of them being latchkey kids.

You really can't leave a child alone who is scared. But dealing with the fears in advance can help to alleviate it, so that by the time you're ready to give it a try, they're no longer scared.

### *They Can Read*

Reading might seem to be a strange skill to have to stay alone, but if you're going to write down rules, phone numbers, and chores, they need to be able to read these things and follow them. Reading is a skill that most kids can have by the time they go to school so it should not be a problem, but do check out your child's reading skills to be sure. There are some kids who are good at hiding learning disabilities, and can't read in fifth grade but have faked their way through.

### *They Make Good Decisions*

When you've let your child make decisions for themselves, were they good ones? If you're not sure, start asking your child what they think about things that could affect their lives and safety before you decide, to find out how your child would act in any situation. Simple choices like when to watch TV, when to do their homework, and which snacks they choose, can be the start of helping them make good choices.

### *They Pay Attention to Others*

If your child is good at helping others and paying attention to others, that's also a good sign that they're self-aware and pay attention. If they don't do that, start pointing out people and things as you go on walks in your neighborhood so that they learn to spot people. For example, if they're walking home from school and a stranger is on the street, you want them to know how to deal with it and to notice in the first place that the stranger is there.

### *They're Aware of Their Surroundings*

Like paying attention to people, they need to be able to pay attention to their surroundings. That's an important skill to have because that's how you notice something burning, or a door that's not locked, or other problems that may arise. They need to know when something is happening that requires a call to a neighbor, a parent, or the police when needed. If they're oblivious to what's going on around them, this could be dangerous for them.

### *Behaves Responsibly*

Does your child behave in responsible ways? If they're still bouncing off the walls and jumping around like a maniac, it could be very dangerous for them to stay home alone. Accidents happen very easily and tossing balls around the house, playing with candles (and fire), and just tumbling around can be very dangerous. If your child still does that when you're around, they are going to do it when they're alone.

### *Shows Their Trustworthiness*

Does your child try to get away with things behind your back? If so, being alone may not be a good thing to do. But, if they're good at being trustworthy and following the rules, it may work. For example, if your child goes with friends, do they ever come home because they thought their friends were misbehaving? That's always a good sign that your child can make mature choices. In contrast, if you're always catching them lying or hiding things, being alone may not be on the cards for them right now.

### *Can Recite Their Home Address and Phone Number*

This is imperative because it will help them get help when they need it. Today, many parents and kids rely on their smartphones to be their memory. But, sometimes these devices do not work. They need to know phone numbers by heart that are important to remember, as well as their own address and possibly the address of someone who can help them if needed.

### *Knows How to Get in Touch with You or Others to Help*

Your child should also know how to get in touch with you on any phone or device. It's better if they don't just know how to use their own cell phone but also how to use other types of phones to get help when needed. It might seem easy to you, but children who were born with smartphones in their hands may not know how to use another type of device.

### *Can Make Simple Snacks Alone*

Usually, after school, a child needs a snack. If they can prepare their own easy snacks such as microwave popped corn, or a sandwich, fruit and so forth, then that makes it easier for them to be home alone. As they get older, they may even be able to start dinner for the family in the evening, which can be an added benefit of teaching children how to care for themselves.

### *Knows How and When to Dial 911*

Another important skill is the ability to call emergency when needed, plus to differentiate when calling 911 is the right thing to do. Having the regular police number as well as the emergency number is a good idea. Having discussions about the difference between a life and death emergency and other types of important situations are very important for everyone. Not being able to fix your snack is not an emergency, for example.

### *Will Follow Instructions and Rules*

If you give your child rules and instructions such as not having friends over, not answering the door, or talking to strangers, you know they'll do what you say. When you leave them a note giving them directions to do something, you know they'll do it. It's imperative that your child follows rules given to them when they're home alone. But remember, if they don't follow them when you're present, they won't follow them when you're not there.

### *Knows Basic First Aid*

If your child skins their knee or stubs their toe or gets a splinter, can they deal with these minor issues themselves? If your child has big reactions to things like this, then you may think twice about leaving them alone. Start working with them to deal with these issues on their own so that they don't feel the need to call you about every scrape.

These skills are important for any child to know when staying home alone. If they fall short and you want them to stay home alone, you will need to train them until they have grasped each of these skills. It's important to teach these skills to kids anyway, but if you are hoping to prepare your child to be a latchkey kid, these skills are more important than ever.

### **Explaining to Your Child What's Happening**

Before you leave your child home alone, you will want to give them time to warm up to the idea, let go of their fears, and develop home alone skills. The best thing that you can do is to take your child's age into consideration. The laws in your area are also important. Follow the law, and then work on preparing your child.

While leaving your child home alone isn't something you probably thought you'd consider, it happens to many. Other children do it safely every day and yours can too. You just need to go about it the right way so that they can be prepared.

### *Explain What Will Happen*

First, consider your child's age and talk to them about staying home alone, and why it's necessary. It's okay to explain that you must work during those hours but that childcare costs a lot of money, and that it would be better to spend that money on other things that you need. If the main reason is that there is no childcare with transportation to and from school, tell them that. Whatever the real reason is that you need to let your child stay home alone after school, explain it to them in words that they understand.

### *Plan Ahead*

There are many scenarios to go over with your child before you leave them alone. By planning for any issue that may arise, you teach them to handle most issues that you didn't even think about. But it takes planning and talking openly and, in an age-appropriate way with your child. Plan the exact snacks your child will have when they're home alone. Plan the activities your child can do when you're not home. If you save some things for only when you're not home, that is going to make them more excited to do it.

### *Set the Rules*

The best thing to do is make very strict rules about what they can do. Be stricter than you normally are. For example, ask them not to answer the phone other than for your parents, grandparents, or other designated people.

Examples of other rules could be: do not tell other people you are alone; do not cook on the stove top; do not climb on counters; do not chat on the internet, and so forth. Make your rules clear not only about what they're not supposed to do but also about exactly what they should do while they're home alone - such as chores, homework, game time, or TV time. Post the rules where your child can read them.

### *Start with Short Stints*

Practice makes perfect. Once you've set the rules and talked to them about everything, start leaving them alone for short periods. For example, run to the store for 30 minutes to see how it goes. When you get back, ask them what they thought about while you were gone and how they felt.

Show up early when they don't expect it too. Test out many scenarios to find out how your child really acts when you're not around. Remember, children's frontal lobes aren't closed yet. This means sometimes they are not good decision makers. Knowing you're there to back them up will help.

***Do a Test Run***

Before you leave them home alone for a longer period regularly, start with a test run. The best test run would involve them unlocking the door and doing everything as if they really were coming home from school alone. Do it around the same time and see how it goes. Be sure to check in with them and find out how they felt about it and whether they have any questions. Walking your child through as many scenarios as possible will help.

***Check In with Your Child***

When your child is alone, be sure to check in with them. The best thing to do is tell them to call you or text you when they get home.

Develop a code word that signals a problem or that they will say if you ask. That way you know it's really them on the text and that they are okay. It'll make you both feel better to know. Some parents ask their child to text them a code word every 20 to 30 minutes just so they know the child is okay.

**Reward Your Children for Good Behavior**

When you get home, if everything looks as it should and after talking to your child you believe they've done a great job, they deserve a reward. You can set up a reward chart that helps encourage them to follow the rules.

You can make a table with the dates, then put star stickers or other stickers in the spaces to show that your child gets a reward for that day. You can add up all the rewards at the end of each week, then set a "reward date" for your child to look forward to. Post the reward chart near the chore list or set up the reward chart as the chore list, so that your child can mark on the reward chart each time they finish or accomplish something.

When you are open with your children about the seriousness of staying home alone and how it's going to work, they're going to be a lot more likely to do a good job. It's important not to hide from them the dangers or your concerns and why it's imperative that they follow your rules.

It's also important to share with them why this is the best choice for your family. That will help mitigate feelings of loneliness or differences with their friends who may do a lot of after-school activities when your child can't due to your situation.

## Setting Up Your Emergency Contact Network

It's important to have a plan in place for emergencies. If your child knows who to call on in different scenarios, that will help. Also, post an emergency call list next to the chore and rule list for your child. One thing to be sure to do is to talk to someone you want to help you with your child in an emergency, or just to help calm their fears.

Be careful about who you tell that your child is home alone too. Sometimes danger lurks behind the face of a friend or family member. In fact, most children who are sexually abused are targeted by someone that they trust such as a coach, an uncle, or a neighbor. The fewer people who know your child is alone, the better.

### *Neighbors*

Before you add any neighbors or friends to your emergency call list, it's imperative to ensure that they give permission. Don't just add people to your emergency list willy-nilly. Even if it's legal in your area for your child to stay alone, you don't want to give nosey people any reason to call child protective services on you. Plus, you want to know for sure that the neighbor is a safe person.

You can learn who in your area is on the sexual predator's list by looking at the Department of Justice's National Sex Offenders public registry. (https://www.nsopw.gov)

### *Relatives*

If you live near family, they are often the best alternatives for your emergency list. But again, make sure it's okay with them because if they can't get to your child during those times, they may be a bad choice. Some relatives may have some serious problems with you leaving your child home, so be sure that you can trust them before you ask them anything.

### *Parents*

This is you and your child's other parent. Even if you're a single parent, having the other parent on the emergency list if they live nearby can be very helpful. Listing your cell number plus work number is an important way to leave the number in case your cell isn't working. Also, teach your child how to ask for people by their actual legal name that they use at work.

### *Older Siblings*

In some cases, a child is staying home alone even though they have older siblings. Leaving that number can be helpful too, if they're available to answer during the time your child is home alone. They can act as eyes and ears for you when needed, but don't put too much pressure on siblings to be babysitters if they work or are in school.

This number, while easily memorable, should be listed too. This way it helps the child remember that they can call that number if needed. Give your child some criteria for calling 911 and explain what happens when they do. Remind them of what 911 will ask when they call so that they know how to answer appropriately without freaking out.

Once you have the list complete, post it near the chore list and the rules list. That way it's all in one spot so that your child knows right where to look. The best place is near a phone; if you want to you can post the numbers near each phone in the house and in each room in the house just in case.

## Setting Boundaries and Expectations for Your Child

Once you've decided that staying home alone is right for your child, even if your child is the most responsible person ever you want to ensure that you set boundaries. Often, these boundaries will be much stronger than if you were home, but when you explain to your child about the whys and reasons, they're going to be a lot more receptive. This is for their protection and the best way to approach this issue.

When you have determined that your child has the physical, emotional, intellectual, and social capability to be a latchkey child, it's up to you to set up the boundaries, expectations, and safety considerations that are important in conjunction with your child. It must be an ongoing discussion and not involve a lot of rules without reason based only on fear.

Some serious boundaries you may want to set include:

### *Telephone Usage*

You will want to instruct your child to contact you when they get home using the home phone. The reason you want them to use the landline is that that's how you know for sure they are in the house. If you don't have a landline, consider getting one for the home for this purpose. The other way to do it is to have them take a picture of themselves in the house in a different spot each day when they get home that you instruct them to do.

This is not about trust; don't frame it in such a way that they feel as if you don't trust them. Frame it as your concern about others taking their phone and pretending to be them, which is why texts without pictures cannot be a good enough way to say they're home. You may also want to implement code words to use in different ways that signal danger or safety. Choose words that aren't likely to be used in normal conversation and that they do not tell others ever.

Additionally, if you let them answer the phone, teach your children to never say that you're not there but to instead take a message because you're busy right now. Then they can send you a text message about the call so that you can return the call fast if it's important.

### *Internet Usage*

The internet in and of itself is not that dangerous. It's how people use it that's the problem. Your child may need the net for watching shows they like, for looking up information for homework, and even talking to their friends.

Depending upon their age, teach them safe internet practices in terms of talking to strangers and letting the public know where they are all the time. This should be par for the course anyway for most kids. But an out-and-out ban may not be appropriate depending on your situation.

One neat thing about the net if you work in a place that can allow this, is that you can actually let them turn on their camera using Skype, Facetime, or Zoom.us (or other streaming option), where it's just on and you can look at your child at any point during the day if you want to, and they can you too.

### *Appliance Usage*

Some ages can probably safely use any type of appliance but for some younger children without the proper dexterity, using knives and fire to cook could be dangerous. Set those boundaries based on their needs and their skill level. Keep teaching them how to use things when you're home so that they can build up to using more appliances safely.

### *The Front Door*

One danger of staying home alone is always the front door. Setting boundaries about who they can allow in, whether they can answer the door, if they can let anyone deliver packages or not, and so forth, is very important. The safety of your neighborhood will dictate a lot of this. You may be okay with your child having one friend over, or you may be okay with them accepting a package, but it will depend on the maturity level of your child and should be something you talk to them about regarding their own comfort level too.

### *Friends*

Many other children are also latchkey kids. There are some parents who believe that a no-company rule is best, and others who are okay with their children having company over to do homework together or play games together. You can always try out different ideas, but for most good kids having a friend over makes them feel safer and won't hurt them.

It does, of course, depend on their age and maturity. But, you do want to check with the other parent to find out how they feel about their child being there without a parent around. They may choose to have your child at their house, or they may be uncomfortable with that.

When you make boundaries for your child, they must be things that you feel good about. If you don't want them talking to anyone, or on the net, or answering the phone or door, that is up to you and something you must choose. But do try to make rules that have reasons behind them that make sense based on your neighborhood, your child, and your situation.

**Dealing with the Unexpected**

One thing to make clear to yourself, your family, your child, and anyone who questions your decision about your child being a latchkey kid, is that it's not neglectful. Sometimes it's very necessary and sometimes it's just what's best for your child. Maybe they are introverts and hate going to group activities after school. Maybe all they want to do is go home and read or play on their computer. That isn't a bad thing.

*Make plans for things that could happen such as:*

- **Being Locked Out** – You know you've done it before too, so it can happen to them. This is not something to be mad about, but it is something to have a plan for. What will your child do if they lose their key or otherwise get locked out? Today you can get doors with fob entry or code entry; is that better in your circumstance or can a neighbor hold a key?

- **Power Outage** – This can be scary for a 30-year-old in the middle of the night, but terrifying for a 9-year-old at 5 pm when it's getting dark in the winter. Talk to your child about power outages, and make sure you have flashlights that work and a plan in place for a power outage. This is a good thing for any family to have anyway.
- **Plumbing Issues** – Everyone gets a clogged toilet or worse, a broken pipe. Teach your child where to turn off the water and who to call if this should happen. The one thing you want to assure your child of is that they're not in trouble if this happens. That way, they know they can ask for help.
- **Broken Glass** – Cleaning up broken glass is dangerous for adults, so make sure your child knows how to do it, or how to hide it from pets so that no one gets hurt and to inform you right away.
- **Fire** – Everyone needs to know what to do in case of fire; namely, get out of the house and call for help. Practice, practice, practice.
- **Bad Weather** – No matter how you plan, the weather has a different one. Teach your child want to do in inclement weather like tornadoes and even floods.

- **First Aid** – It's important that your child know basic first aid. You can sign them up for a class for children that will teach them what to know. Keep a good first aid kit in your home too and let them know where it is.

When you set your child up for success, nothing can be neglectful about it. You're teaching your child important skills for life that you may not have taught them without considering them being a latchkey kid. Latchkey kids are self-sufficient, smart, and self-motivated. What could be better for helping them prepare for what's coming? Adulthood.

Printed by Libri Plureos GmbH in Hamburg, Germany